DEMOCRACY AND SOCIALISM
IN CHINA

DEMOCRACY AND SOCIALISM
IN CHINA

DEMOCRACY AND SOCIALISM IN CHINA

Su Shaozhi

in discussion with
Michael Barratt Brown, Wlodzimierz Brus,
John Eaton and Andras Hegedüs

Spokesman

First published in 1982
by Spokesman
Bertrand Russell House
Gamble Street
Nottingham NG7 4ET

British Library Cataloguing in Publication Data

Shaozhi, Su
Socialist democracy and development in China.
1. China — Politics and government — 1949 —
I. Title
951.05   DS777.55

ISBN 0-85124-343-6

This book is copyright under the Berne Convention. All rights are strictly reserved. No part of this publication may be reproduced or transmitted in any form or by any means without permission

Copyright © Spokesman, 1982

Printed by the Russell Press Ltd., Nottingham

Contents

Foreword *by Ken Coates* 7

I. Some Questions in China's Socialist Economic Construction — *Su Shaozhi* 9

II. Some Questions — *Wlodzimierz Brus* 33

III. Some Comments — *John Eaton* 36

IV. Some Comments — *Andras Hegedüs* 41

V. Some Comments — *Michael Barratt Brown* 45

VI. A Short Reply — *Su Shaozhi* 50

VII. Science & Technology and Democratisation in Socialist Development Strategies — *Su Shaozhi* 59

Foreword

Professor Su Shaozhi was a distinguished guest in Rome, at a seminar on Bukharin which was organised by the Istituto Gramsci in 1980. This was a profoundly interesting meeting, with scholarly papers from a variety of Marxist and non-Marxist thinkers. Many of us spent much of our time in Frattocchie, the flower-strewn seat of the Gramsci Institute's chosen conference centre, talking through the nights with our Chinese colleague.

I was therefore very happy to meet him again within months, at the Yugoslavian Conference on *Socialism in the World,* in Cavtat. Here Su Shaozhi presented the paper which forms the basis of this book. Other Cavtat papers will be published after this little volume, but we should thank the Yugoslav sponsors of this forum for their initiative in opening this (and many another) discussion. After leaving Cavtat, I reported on it to the Russell Foundation, which agreed to circulate Professor Su's paper for comments, inviting various economists to offer their views on it.

Of course, there are great difficulties involved in the relationship between planning and democracy, and we do not for a moment believe that the papers published here can offer more than the beginning of a dialogue which all of us hope will extend itself considerably. Socialist ideas in China are of enormous interest in Europe, even though there is a general apprehension of major cultural and historical differences which can change the meaning of apparently common terms, and render true communication very difficult. However difficult it may be, no-one can doubt that the effort is both urgent and rewarding.

The Russell Foundation offers these pages as the opening chapter in what it hopes will become an extensive and long-running exchange.

Ken Coates

I

Some Questions in China's Socialist Economic Construction

Su Shaozhi

The situation in China as a whole has been developing rapidly after the overthrow of the "gang of four" in October 1976 and particularly after the Third Plenary Session of the Eleventh Central Committee of the Chinese Communist Party in December 1978. Fundamental changes have taken place and tremendous progress has been made in the economic, political, cultural and educational fields.

These changes and progress were heralded by an ideological prerequisite . . . the nationwide discussion of the criterion of truth, which began in May 1978. Through discussion it has been clearly affirmed that "practice is the sole criterion for testing truth", which is a consistent basic principle of the Marxist theory of knowledge, as opposed to dogmatism, personality cult, ideological ossification and procccding in all things from books; it stands for emancipating the mind, using one's brain, seeking truth from facts, linking theory with practice and proceeding in all things from reality. As a result, the Marxist dialectical materialist ideological line is revived, which provides the conditions for us to break down all dogmas and superstitions, earnestly sum up past experience, develop the strong points and correct mistakes, reform the economic system and try to find a correct path of socialist construction which is suited to the characteristics of our country and the particularities of the times.

A Brief Review of China's Socialist Construction in the Past Thirty Years

After the victory of the Chinese revolution in 1949, China's national economic development has in the main gone through five stages.

1. The period of restoration of the national economy and the period of the First Five-Year Plan.

Despite our lack of experience during this period, we realistically proceeded from the actual conditions, more or less respected the objective laws and paid particular attention to overall balance. In less than three years, the wounds of long years of war were healed, and the financial and economic situation made a fundamental turn for the better. In 1956 the socialist transformation of the ownership of the means of production was basically completed, and the exploiting class was basically eliminated as a class. The First Five-Year Plan was fulfilled ahead of time, the economy grew at considerable speed and the achievement was great. The Eighth National Congress of the Chinese Communist Party convened in 1956 laid down a correct Party line and tasks, which were the correct handling of contradictions among the people, bringing every positive factor into play, vigorously developing the productive forces and building China into a great socialist country. The shortcoming in this period was that the experience of other countries was copied indiscriminately and not fully integrated with China's actual conditions.

2. The period of "the Great Leap Forward" and three years of economic difficulties.

In 1956 it was proposed that we find a road of economic development suitable to China's conditions, so that we would be able to achieve more, faster, better and more economical results, which later became a famous slogan. The aspiration was good. But the magnified struggle against the Rightists in 1957 (those wrongly designated as Rightists were all rehabilitated in 1979) and the struggle against "Right deviation" in the economic field impaired the principle of seeking truth from facts and doing things according to one's capability, and the symptoms of a "Left" trend cropped up. In "the Great Leap Forward" and the movement for organising the People's Communes proposed in 1958, it became common practice to put forward impossibly high production quotas, give arbitrary and impracticable directions and stir up a "communist wind". The idea of using the mass movement as a means to build China into a strong country within the shortest possible time and effect the "transition" to communism as quickly as possible went against objective laws and actually prevented us from reaching the goal. It resulted in "Left" deviationist mistakes, serious economic imbalance, extremely heavy losses and three years of economic difficulties.

3. The period of readjustment of the national economy.

The seriousness of the situation was perceived in the latter half of 1960. In the latter half of 1961, the policy of eight characters . . . readjustment, consolidation, filling out and raising standards . . . was put forward and effectively implemented. The national economy entered into a period of readjustment. A series of measures were adopted, including sufficiently reducing the scale of industry, rearranging production according to manpower and material and financial resources, and leaving no "gaps" in the economic plans, in order to overcome the "Leftist" errors in the economic work. As these measures were in accord with the objective economic laws, the economic situation turned for the better. Production increased and the market prospered. By 1965-66, the economic situation had once again become favourable. But there were mistakes too in this period. In the economic field, although great setbacks had been suffered, the bitter experience had not been summed up and the "Leftist" thinking in running the economy had not been refuted. A theoretical mistake was in the assessment put forward in 1968 that "classes and class struggle exist throughout the historical period of socialism", an assessment which negated the correct conclusion reached at the Eighth National Congress of the Party that after 1956, class struggle was no longer the principal contradiction of socialism. In 1965 the term "capitalist roaders", an unscientific concept, was coined, and it was erroneously maintained that the basic theory and basic practice in the years after the founding of the

People's Republic were made up by the struggle between the two classes and two roads. This prepared the theoretical grounds for the coming "great cultural revolution".

4. The period of the "great cultural revolution".

When the national economy was making a favourable turn and the country was accumulating some strength, the "great cultural revolution" broke out of the blue. The assessment made at the time of the situation in the Party and the country as a whole was contrary to reality. The principle of democratic centralism was departed from and wrong ways and policies of struggle were adopted. Lin Biao and the "gang of four" and their like made use of the serious mistakes, partially usurped the power of the Party and the state, created and pursued an ultra-Left line. They wholly negated the achievements made in the previous period of economic readjustment, opposed the principle of "to each according to his work" and economic accounting, were against economic specialisation and co-ordination, international trade and international economic co-operation. They even tried to replace the development of the productive forces with class struggle, throwing the industrial and commercial enterprises and the countryside into a chaotic mess. Industrial and agricultural production suffered serious damage, and the national economy was pushed to the verge of total collapse. A great disaster fell upon the heads of the Chinese people.

5. The new period of building a powerful socialist country with modern agriculture, industry, national defence and science and technology.

After the "gang of four" was smashed in October 1976 and the ultra-Left line and trend of Lin Biao and the "gang of four" were repudiated, the national economy began to recover and grow. And yet in the period immediately after the overthrow of the "gang of four", some erroneous formulations were not corrected, such as "classes and class struggle exist throughout the historical period of socialism" and "taking class struggle as the key link", and the damage wrought by Lin Biao and the "gang of four" was underestimated. The trend of "going at it in a big way" and "going after higher targets" in the economy was not rectified, and many problems existed in the national economy. China did not embark upon a correct road of socialist construction until the correct political and ideological line of the Party was fully re-established at the Third Plenary Session of the Eleventh Central Committee of the Chinese Communist Party. The plenary session set forth the task of building China into a powerful, modernised socialist country, reiterating that the large-scale and turbulent class struggles of the masses have in the main come to an end and that the whole Party and the whole country must shift the focal point of work on to economic construction, and proposed that a good job must be done in readjusting, restructuring, consolidating and improving the national economy in the next few years as the first battle in the march towards the four modernisations. It stood for promoting democracy, emancipating people's minds, summing up experience, proceeding on the basis of China's reality, and drawing up long-term plans and five-year plans. It called for solving problems left over from the past, fostering socialist democracy and strengthening the socialist legal system, so that China will be able to embark upon a correct road of socialist construction.

In the past thirty years we have achieved tremendous successes. We have set up the state power of the dictatorship of the proletariat led by the working class and based on the worker/peasant alliance, eliminated the system of exploitation, built up independent and fairly comprehensive industrial and economic systems, promoted science, education and culture in the interest of the people. But as a result of the two setbacks, the development of the national economy was disrupted and valuable time was lost.

THE BASIC LESSONS TO BE LEARNED FROM THE THIRTY YEARS OF ECONOMIC CONSTRUCTION

We have learned from achievements and setbacks in the past thirty years of economic construction, which have taught us some profound lessons. To generalise, we have, I think, come to understand the following basic points:

1. The basic aim of the socialist revolution is to liberate the productive forces, continually raise labour productivity and meet the needs of the people in their material and cultural life. After the proletariat has obtained political power in the whole country, it must steadfastly shift the focus of its

work to economic construction, vigorously develop the productive forces and gradually improve the livelihood of the people if no large-scale war breaks out.

2. After the proletariat has gained political power, it must make a scientific analysis of the state of the classes in the country and the class struggle, an analysis based on the current stage of social development and in conformity with the objective reality, and adopt correct policies and measures to maintain the necessary political stability. After the basic completion of the socialist transformation of the ownership of the means of production in China, the exploiting class in China was eliminated as a class. Although class struggle still exists within a certain scope, it must never be magnified, still less staging man-made class struggle. It is necessary to prevent all attempts to shift the centre of work away from economic construction and allow "political movements" and "class struggle", which hurt the development of productive forces, to interfere.

3. Voluntarism must be opposed in building socialism; efforts must be made to do things according to objective laws (including economic laws and laws of nature). As far as economic laws are concerned, the first and foremost law is that production relations must be suited to the nature of the productive forces; no attempt is to be made to change the mode of production relations prematurely and overtake the productive forces. Next comes the basic economic law of socialism. It must be made clear that the aim of socialist production is to satisfy to the utmost limit the needs of

the people in their material and cultural life; it should not be production for the sake of production, or production for the sake of reaching higher targets. The third is the law of planned and proportionate development. In economic planning, overall balance must be carefully maintained so as to establish proper ratios between the various departments of the national economy, between accumulation and consumption, between scientific, cultural and educational undertakings on the one hand and economic construction as a whole on the other. It is impermissible to one-sidedly go after the growth of one department, such as iron and steel. The fourth is the law of "to each according to his work." It is necessary to recognise the principle of material incentive, uphold the principle of "to each according to his work, more pay for more work, and he who does not work, neither shall he eat", and oppose equalitarianism. The fifth is the law of value. As production in China at the present stage is still commodity production, it is necessary to recognise the regulating role of the law of value to a certain extent in production and circulation, and oppose managing the economy solely by administrative methods in place of economic methods. There are, of course, more objective economic laws to be adhered to. The above are the relatively more important ones.

4. To carry out economic construction, it is essential to proceed from China's realities and never from books and treat Marxist theories as dogmas. In no case should foreign experience be blindly copied. The most prominent reality in China is that China is the most populous country in

the world and its productive forces and socialized production are still at a very low level of development. One must not depart from this starting point when studying China's socialist construction.

5. Today when science and technology are developing by leaps and bounds, modernization is out of the question if a country does not participate in international economic intercourse. For this reason, the policy of self-reliance must not be one-sidedly and rigidly understood, and by no means should a policy of closing the country against all international contact be adopted.

6. Socialist construction must be ensured by democracy, political democracy and economic democracy. This is a highly important question which is closely linked with promoting the enthusiasm and initiative of the masses of the people, with opposing bureaucracy and preventing power from over-concentrating in the hands of a few, resulting in individuals making arbitrary decisions. The working people must have the right to take part in the administration of the country and management of the enterprises.

EXPLORING THE WAY OF CHINA'S SOCIALIST CONSTRUCTION

The socialist society, like all other societies, has to go through a process of development from the lower to the higher stage. The first stage of communism envisaged by Marx in his *Critique of the Gotha Programme* may be regarded as socialism in its higher and matured stage. China before liberation was a poor and backward semi-colonial and semi-feudal society with a huge population where small-scale peasant economy prevailed and natural economy occupied the dominant position. It had no socialised large-scale production to provide it with a material basis, and it had not experienced bourgeois democracy. After the proletariat won political power it therefore needed a relatively long period of transition before entering into socialism. After the basic completion of the socialist transformation of the ownership of the means of production, China is still a developing country, its socialist system is still imperfect and its economy and culture under-developed. It is still a country with a huge population but a meagre economic foundation. These are the realities of China.

Acting in accordance with the principle that practice is the sole criterion for testing truth, summing up the experience and lessons of the past thirty years of socialist construction, proceeding from China's realities and at the same time learning from the positive and negative experience of other countries, China is exploring and gradually forming a correct road of socialist construction in conformity with China's realities, which is usually known as the Chinese road of modernisation.

1. Building a Powerful Socialist Country with the Four Modernisations is our Firm Objective

The Eleventh National Congress of the Party and the First Session of the Fifth National People's Congress both set the goal of achieving the modernisation of our agriculture, industry, national defence and science and technology by the end of the century; the Third Plenary Session of the

Eleventh Central Committee of the Party and the Second Session of the Fifth National People's Congress decided to shift the focus of the work of the whole Party and the whole nation to socialist modernisation, beginning from 1979; the Fifth Plenary Session of the Eleventh Party Central Committee resolved that no time was to be lost to speedily solve such important questions as laying down long-term plans of national economic development and deciding on economic systems that are suited to the needs of national economic growth. The task now facing us is to unite the people of all nationalities and bring into play all positive factors so that we can work with one heart and one mind, develop the socialist economy in a planned and proportionate way to achieve greater, faster, better and more economical results, and build a modernised, highly democratic, highly civilised, powerful, socialist country.

The realisation of the four modernisations means gradually turning China's agriculture into a well-developed agricultural system with a rational distribution and all-round development of farming, forestry, animal husbandry, side-line occupations and fisheries to meet the needs of the people and of an expanding industry. It means enabling the rural areas gradually to grow into rich bases combining agriculture, industry and commerce. It means gradually turning our industry into an advanced industrial system which is complete in range and rational in structure and which meets the needs of consumers and the expansion of the whole economy. It means enabling China's science and technology to approach or catch up with advanced world levels. It means that China will raise its national defence capabilities concommitantly with her economic development and be strong enough to defend its security and resist and defeat foreign aggressors in case of a modern war. In the course of modernisation, China will gradually take its place in the front ranks of the world in terms of gross national product and output of major products, so that our people will enjoy stable and gradual improvement in their material and cultural well-being as production increases. It is estimated that by the end of this century the average percapita gross national product will be increased to about US $1,000, that is, four times the present figure.

2. *Do a Good Job in Readjusting the National Economy*

We are at present engaged in readjusting, restructuring, consolidating and improving the national economy. First of all, a good job must be done in the readjustment. As a result of the sabotage by Lin Biao and the "gang of four", the disproportionality in our national economy is still very serious. Serious confusions still exist in production, capital construction, circulation and distribution. Readjustment, therefore, means readjusting the proportional relations. This includes the proportional relations between agriculture and industry, within agriculture itself and industry itself, between accumulation and consumption; it also includes curtailing the scale of capital construction and changing impractically high targets.

We are concentrating our efforts on developing

agriculture as quickly as possible. The Central Committee issued two documents concerning policies in the rural areas, which include raising the purchasing prices of farm products, giving the production teams genuine power to make their own decisions, and implementing the policy of simultaneous development of farming, forestry, animal husbandry, side-line occupations and fisheries comprehensively and according to circumstances. The peasants' initiative for production has been greatly raised, and agricultural production has increased more speedily.

In industry, the development of light and textile industries has been accelerated, enabling them to grow at a faster rate than the heavy industry. In the heavy industry, the development of energy, transport and communications, and construction has been strengthened. In our national economic plans today, priority is given in the following order: energy, transport and communications, construction, agriculture, light industries and the heavy industry. We have also more realistically decided on the rate of growth in industrial production, giving special attention to the quality, variety and specifications of the products and seeing that they meet the needs of the people.

Between accumulation and consumption, we have appropriately and gradually reduced the proportion of accumulation. Most economists maintain that 25 per cent of the national income is a more or less suitable figure for accumulation. As production increases, the living standard of the people is to be gradually improved, including higher personal income and better living conditions, such as building more houses.

Capital construction is curtailed on the one hand in a number of projects where it is necessary and possible, and on the other in investment, so that the scale of capital construction undertaken by the state will correspond to the present manpower, financial and material resources of the state.

In the course of readjustment, problems to be solved also include enlarging the commercial network, developing the service trade, expanding international trade and tourism, and dealing with the questions of employment, family planning, wages policy and price adjustments.

Fairly good results have been achieved in less than two years of economic readjustment. But there are still some problems, which have to be solved in restructuring the economic system.

3. Orientation in Restructuring the Economic System

As we carry out economic readjustment, we are confronted with a big problem . . . that the present economic system does not suit the development of the economy. This calls for a gradual reform of the present economic system.

We hold that the realisation of present reforms in the economic system can be regarded as another reform of historical importance in the relations of production, following the basic completion of the socialist transformation in the ownership of the means of production in 1956.

As investigation, study and experiments in selected places in connection with reform of the economic system are still under way, experience is being continually summed up; and as there are many complicated problems, there is not yet a complete set of programmes and measures. However, the experiments made at selected places in less than two years and their successes show that some assumptions, when applied, yield satisfactory results. This has clarified the orientation of reform in the following aspects.

1. In the ownership of the means of production one of the basic features of socialism is the change from private ownership into public ownership. But whether a mode of ownership of the means of production is good or bad should not be judged by its degree of public ownership; it should be judged by whether it can promote the development of the productive forces or not. Under China's conditions, ownership of the means of production by the whole people (which is, in fact, ownership by the state at the present stage), and ownership by collectives and individual working people who do not exploit others will co-exist for a fairly long period of time and develop side by side. This is in keeping with China's present level of development of the productive forces. Since China is a country where the productive forces are under-developed and economic development is unbalanced, employment constitutes a considerable problem. In the cities, employment opportunities will be multiplied if besides ownership by the whole people, there is also collective ownership, and different forms of collective ownership at that, and at the same time, if individual working people, who do not exploit others, are allowed to exist. In the rural areas, collective ownership is firmly established in the great

majority of places. In some sparsely populated, economically backward and poor areas, a production responsibility system closely linked with output, including the fixing of output quotas based on a group or a household, can be implemented, and private-plot economy and other forms of auxiliary economy should be allowed greater development. This will liven up the economy. Of course, this does not means that individual working people do not have to organise themselves into collectives. What is meant is that collectivisation should be an inevitable demand as the productive forces develop; it should be done truly voluntarily, not enforced from above by administrative orders.

2. In distribution, there is a long-standing problem in which the material benefits received by an enterprise or a worker have nothing to do with whether the enterprise is successfully or poorly managed or whether the worker makes greater or smaller contribution in his or her work. This places great restrictions on the initiative of the enterprises and individual workers and on raising labour productivity. We must acknowledge that the principle of material gains is a basic historical materialist principle and that the principle of "to each according to his work" linked with material incentives is a socialist law governing the distribution of consumer goods for the individual. In China at present, material interest involves a three-sided relationship between the state (central and local governments), the collective enterprises and the working individuals; and the interests of the three sides must be correctly linked. There should be a difference in remuneration and income to be

received by enterprises which are well managed and those poorly managed, and individuals who work well and those who do not work well. It is necessary to implement a system of "to each according to his work and more pay for more work", including adopting piece wages and a bonus system, and to encourage a part of the people and regions to become well-off first as a result of receiving more income for more work.

3. In the relationship between planning and the market, we acknowledge on the one hand that socialist production is a planned economy, which is determined by the public ownership of the means of production. On the other hand, we also acknowledge that socialist production is still commodity production in which both the means of subsistence and the means of production are commodities. This is because in our society there is still ownership by the whole people, collective ownership and working individuals in the interests of the whole people, the enterprises and the individuals, and the interests of the three cannot be well coordinated without commodity production. We have therefore changed the view which places planning in opposition to the market. We have come to understand that while planned development is impossible without state planning, the economy cannot be rationally organised without regulation by the market. It has been suggested that under the guidance of state planning, regulation by the market must be made full use of. Once the regulating role of the market is acknowledged, it is necessary to acknowledge the regulating role of the law of value to a certain extent and permit a certain

degree of competition.

4. In the economic system, we in the past one-sidedly understood a planned economy as making all-inclusive and compulsory plans from above. The result was that the economy was placed under excessive and rigid control and that as the economy was administered according to the administrative system, areas and levels and by administrative methods, power was over concentrated, which often gave rise to bureaucracy and violation of the objective economic laws. The enterprises themselves had no power to make decisions and had to wait for assignment from and approval by the higher levels in everything. The tightly fettered enterprises were answerable only to the higher levels and the plans and were alienated from the market and the needs of the people. Consequently their products were unsalable, resulting in huge stockpiling, losses on the part of the enterprises and great waste. Hence the proposal to give the enterprises greater power to make decisions, break the bounds of the different departments and administrative areas, separate the economic management system from the administrative system, that is, abolish the method of combining the party, government and enterprise into one, organise the economy according to economic laws and manage the economy by economic methods. Organising the economy according to economic laws requires that the enterprises specialise and co-ordinate, give play to the advantage of the localities, organise all forms of integration, develop commodity production and realise and enlarge the socialisation of production. Managing the economy by economic

methods requires the state to regulate the economy by making full use of the regulating role of the market and such factors in the commodity and monetary relations as profits, wages, taxation and interest, and makes it necessary for an enterprise to be responsible for its own profits and losses and handle its own finances in the future on the basis of greater decision-making power.

5. In the structure of the national economy, we one-sidedly emphasised over a long period in the past the importance of giving priority to the development of heavy industry and "taking steel as the key link" thought little of specialisation and co-ordination. As a result we built a large number of "big and all-embracing" and "small and all-embracing" enterprises, creating irrationality in the structure of our economy. This was manifested in disproportionality between industry and agriculture, within industry and agriculture and between accumulation and consumption, over-extended capital construction, the construction of too many duplicate enterprises, low utilisation ratio of equipment and acute employment problems. It is therefore necessary to work hard to achieve overall balance, curtail capital construction, arrange the national economic plan in the order of energy, transport and communications, construction, agriculture, light industry and heavy industry, and to develop the service trade in a big way, so as to enable the various departments of the national economy to develop in harmony and co-ordination, achieve rational distribution of production, make full and efficient use of the manpower, material and financial resources and

natural resources, carry on social reproduction without obstruction and promote a faster development of socialist construction.

6. On the basis of self-reliance we are to learn from the advanced experience of foreign countries, energetically import and make use of advanced techniques of other countries and fully utilise foreign investments. In the world today, when science and technology are developing at a swift pace and when there is steadily closer economic contact between countries, international trade, mutual import and utilisation of advanced technology and the use of foreign capital in construction are normal economic intercourse between countries and necessary conditions for realising modernisation. China has laid down a policy of utilising foreign capital, which developed from buying foreign advanced techniques, machinery and equipment to accepting foreign loans and then to permitting foreigners to invest in and set up, within a certain scope, joint ventures of Chinese and foreign investment. This is an important measure to hasten the realisation of modernisation and greatly increase China's capabilities to rely on itself. We have also investigated and studied the theories, methods, experience and lessons concerning economic reform carried out by other countries, which of course can be used only for reference and should not be mechanically copied. We must study earnestly ourselves and find an economic system that meets the needs in developing the productive forces in China.

7. Without democracy there is no socialism; without democracy there are no four modernisa-

tions. To promote socialist democracy and improve the socialist legal system are important topics that confront us at present. The masses of the working people are the masters of the country and the enterprises. It is therefore important to ensure that the people truly have the power to manage the affairs of the state and the enterprises. It is an important factor for preventing the evils of bureaucracy.

China was for a long time a feudal autocratic country. Our cadres and people have been more deeply influenced by feudalism than by capitalism. To promote socialist democracy it is therefore necessary for the cadres and people to free themselves from the pernicious influence of feudal despotism and the force of habit of the small producers. As a socialist country it is imperative to establish a fundamental democratic system, earnestly practise democratic centralism, oppose patriarchism, prevent power from concentrating in the hands of a few, place the cadres of various levels truly under the supervision of the people of the whole country, and create a really lively and vigorous political life. The Chinese Communist Party is studying how to genuinely solve the problem of democratic centralism in terms of the system of the Party and the state. It has set up disciplinary committees and decided to abolish the *de facto* system of life-long terms of office for cadres. It is laid down in China's Constitution in clear terms that "the state adheres to the principle of socialist democracy, and ensures to the people the right to participate in the management of state affairs and of all economic and cultural undertakings, and the right to supervise the organs of state and their personnel".

To ensure that the people take part in managing the affairs of the state, it has been reiterated that the rights of citizens defined in the Constitution are to be firmly protected. Laws like the Organic Law of the Local People's Congresses and the Local People's Government of the People's Republic of China and the Electoral Law for the National People's Congress and Local People's Congresses of the People's Republic of China have been promulgated to ensure and facilitate the people of the whole country to participate in the management of the affairs of the state and exercise effective supervision over the state organs and functionaries.

Socialist democracy in the enterprises is embodied in democratic management. The basic form of democratic management in the enterprises in China at present is the workers' congress under the leadership of the Party committee. The workers' congress is democratically elected by the entire staff and workers of an enterprise. As it has the deepest roots in the masses, it can reflect the opinion of the masses on an extensive basis. Through this organised and guided form, the workers' congress can regularly discuss and examine all the important questions concerning the enterprise, including the important production plans, management, organisation of labour, finances, welfare and labour protection. It can make the necessary resolutions and pass them on to those concerned in the enterprises for execution. The workers' congress in an enterprise or a workshop can also assess, supervise and elect the leading personnel at the basic levels of the enterprise. It can successfully play the role of an organ of power, of the staff and workers, to manage the enterprise and foster democracy in politics, techniques, economy and daily life.

The capitalist system has existed for more than three hundred years. Although it has created tremendous productive forces, it has inevitably met with many failures, setbacks and crises in the course of its development. Today, it is still harassed by repeated political and economic crises. The socialist system does not have a very long history. It is inevitable that in the course of its development there are complications and zigzags. But fundamentally, the socialist system has an incomparable superiority over the capitalist system. Only the socialist system can overcome the insurmountable and innate contradictions of the capitaist system, make the identity of the fundamental interest of the people a fact, give full play to the initiative and creativeness of the working people, develop the social productive forces in a planned and proportionate way and at a high speed, and satisfy the growing needs of all the members of society in their material and cultural life. The cause of socialism is pressing ahead; it will gradually win victory in the whole world through voluntary choice by the people of various countries and through a road suited to the characteristics of their own countries.

II

Some Questions
Wlodzimierz Brus

1. I find the paper very interesting, informative and stimulating. It raises a number of questions, the importance of which goes beyond China and her route of socialist construction. I find myself in particular agreement with two points made on pages 17 and 18 (points 4 and 6) about the needs to "proceed from China's realities and never from books" and that "socialist construction must be ensured by democracy, political democracy and economic democracy". There are many other points which I share (e.g. about the need and the concept of economic reforms, the position of agriculture, the combination of state-collective and private ownership of means of production), but the above two seem of paramount significance.

2. It is, however, not enough to recognise verbally the indispensability of democratic participation — an effort must be made to chart the ways of implementation of the principle. It is obvious from the paper what were the undemocratic sources of *past* mistakes (disasters actually); they never arrived "out of the blue" as the author writes about the cultural revolution, they always came as a result of unqualified condemnation of someone

elses' policies and equally unqualified praise for the *current* policies, leaders etc.; in other words the right to express views different from those currently prevailing is an essential element of preventing the repetition of past history. It would be therefore most valuable for getting a truly Marxist perspective of Chinese socialist development if the author would be able to discuss in more concrete terms the ways and means of such a change in political set-up in the framework of "China's realities". I emphasise that references to economic democracy won't exhaust the problem: it is not decisions about production in enterprises which I have in mind (although they are important), but the possibility of public control over policies and decisions on a national scale and over personal composition of the leading political bodies.

3. One of the basic conditions for making use of pragmatic thinking instead of rigid clichés seems to me to be the realisation that there are no ideal solutions, that is to say that by opting for a particular solution we should be aware also of the possible negative consequences which have to be minimised. This means that in advancing new policies we should *openly* discuss *problems* associated with them. As I said, I am in favour of most of the new policies presented in the paper, but almost in every case I would see dangers and pitfalls as well. The author seems to have glossed over this aspect — so maybe the balance could be redressed. I shall give some examples:

The economic reform is expected to have a positive impact on productivity: how does this relate to the grave problem of securing full employment?

The economic reform assumes a substantial change in the role of prices, among other things a much greater price flexibility: how is this to be reconciled with the deeply ingrained conviction of the over-riding priority of price stability?

The economic reform assumes a greater role of the market mechanism, which, in principle, can be reconciled with central planning. But this is not an easy job, especially in a country like China where some of the market ingredients of a Soviet-type system (full consumer market and full labour market) are missing.

The stress on material incentives is understandable, but does this mean to "oppose equalitarianism" as the author writes? Is the distribution policy to be completely "purified" from any social objectives, is it a matter of keeping differentials within some set of constraints? I can't believe that a move from one extreme to another is what the present Chinese policy has in mind. But if not — conflicts between different aspects are inevitable and they have to be discussed.

There are many other points which could gain very much from a many-sided examination.

III

Some Comments
John Eaton

It is a great pleasure to have an opportunity to read and comment on Comrade Su Shaozhi's paper. There is today far too little free and frank exchange of ideas between socialists in different countries and yet, from when the socialist movement was coming into being up till the first two or three decades of this century, trustful and open internationalism was of the very essence of socialism itself.

I was particularly interested in the summary of the five stages of China's economic development; I myself was associated with some of the first developments of China/Britain trade in stage number one and this still seems to me something of a "golden age"! Relationships then seemed very open and simple — many excellent people were then co-operating, without inhibitions or fears, to find commonsense solutions to elementary problems of putting basic components of the economy into some sort of running order. People then used their intelligence and devotion to the cause of liberation to very good effect and China won a wide circle of warm friends abroad, in Britain, in India, throughout the whole world. Some very important and lasting foundation stones for a democratic society, a new, people's society were then laid: the stark misery, degradation and gangsterism from which Chinese society had so long suffered, gave place to a society in which almost everyone could meet his or her elemental needs in terms of food, clothing and shelter and almost everyone had some part to play in the life of society, some useful work to do and some say in how work should be arranged and for what ends. Peasants, for example, who had long been victims of arbitrary exploitation acquired some dignity and status as human beings.

Perhaps there is still something to learn from these early years following Liberation in 1949. Social and economic aims were elemental but fairly clear, simple and obvious. What economic aims should be as development takes place is often a very difficult question to answer — even in theoretical terms and even more so in practice. What content is one to give, for example, to such words as "construction", "productivity" or "modernisation"? What material things and what patterns of economic relationships between people, what knowledge and experience in those who are engaged in production are needed to realise the goal we describe as socialist construction? If raising productivity means more outputs relative to inputs, we need to ask 'Output of what?' and 'Input of what?' Do we just want what is already being produced but more of it? A new mix of products? Altogether new products? If a new mix, what new mix? If new products, what new products? And which 'inputs' should we most urgently strive to save — labour, energy, materials or what? Does 'modernisation' mean acquiring and using modern science and knowledge? If so, one must ask, 'What kind of science, knowledge of what?'; for without asking such questions there is a danger of imitating very bad forms of science and technology such as some of those that have been developed in 'industrially advanced' countries of the West.

All these are very difficult questions to answer and it is my belief every effort should be made to let the people most affected by the answers find their own answers for themselves. Otherwise they will blame others for what they don't like. Also they themselves best know their own preferences. When they make mistakes they themselves will learn from these mistakes and also be in a position to correct their own mistakes. However, when one talks of people in an economic context, one must mean 'groups of people' since production and distribution are *social* activities. Preferences are, of course, choices by individuals but individuals can only effectively express themselves by taking part in and influencing decisions from within the groups of which they form a part. Devolution of decision making whenever it is socially and economically possible to do so is important, not only because people resent suffering from mistakes imposed upon them from outside, from other people, but when they have a chance to use their own capacities and learn from their experiences. Collective wisdom *when it can be harnessed* will always be wiser than the wisest of individuals.

If the lines of thought I have sketched above have any validity the point that Comrade Su makes his Section 3 — "Basic Lessons" — seems to be very important: ". . . The first and foremost law is that production relations must be suited to the nature of the productive forces; no attempt is to be made to change the mode of production relations prematurely and overtaking the productive forces . . .". I think this means that one must respect the existing ways in which economic problems are coped with socially. If cloth is being woven, it must continue to be woven. One must be careful not to go over to new methods until one is sure that they will work. But the people best able to judge whether existing methods are working adequately or whether the time has come for change, are the producers themselves. So the guiding thread of economic policy should be at all levels, national, regional, district and 'at the grass roots', in individual factories and communities, to serve the two-fold aims of (1) keeping the economy functioning as regards essentials and (2) introducing changes only with the approval of those who have to make them work and those who are significantly affected by them. To achieve such objectives I believe it is necessary always to seek means of as far as possible devolving control over economic decisions; for example, if only a smallish local or sectoral group will be significantly affected by a decision of a particular kind, then seek to make provisions so that such decisions be taken by the group in its own way for itself. All this is easier said than done but I am coming to the view that socialist economic policy making is primarily about levels at which decisions can be taken and that national policy should limit itself to as few as possible centrally taken decisions and create an ever widening living space for creative initiatives and decision taking on the part of producers and consumers themselves

IV

Some Comments

Andras Hegedüs

I would like to start by confessing that I am far from being an expert on China so my reflections take the form of a confrontation of Eastern European experiences with the these of Su Shaozhi.

1. The periodisation given by the author for the development of China's national economy is very important and easy to comprehend. But this periodization does not enable us to distinguish changes in the institutional system and changes in political direction and the economic policies involved. As far as Eastern Europe in concerned, this distinction seems to be very important: fundamental changes in the institutional system came into being only in Yugoslavia where the Stalinist state management system was succeeded by a self-management system, while in other Eastern European countries we can observe only the changes in the political course, e.g. Khrushchevism, Kádárism, etc.

2. In Eastern European experience these changes could be traced back to different interests of social strata and to the struggle between different social groups. With a social/scientific approach the cause of these changes should not be

sought only in the failures or achievements of certain politicians or political groups. I appreciate the author's embitterment against Lin Biao and the "gang of four" but it does not free us from the task of looking for the deeper causes of the ultra-left line, and its ascendance at the time, which are to be found in the antagonism to the bureaucracy existing among the masses.

3. Surely the changes that have taken place in China since 1976 have a very important bearing on the issue of socialism, but the Marxist social sciences must look at these changes with a critical eye. Eastern European experience has shown that apologetics for the prevailing political course restrain the process of renewal and movement for reform. A critical analysis must pinpoint not only the objective but also the negative subjective factors. Involved in the latter are the contradictions and imperfections of the power structure.

4. In the paper there is a stress on the importance of the development of democracy. In Eastern Europe, sociologists have demonstrated how the participation of workers in the state-management system and their activity in the self-management system can become merely formal. For this reason, it is important for the critical Marxist social sciences to search for institutional safeguards against such formalisation. In Poland the problem of self-management has been raised.

5. It is an exciting idea that the primary aim is to create a well-developed agricultural system in China and that industrial development must be oriented to this. Alongside, there is the question of the development of light and heavy industry.

Eastern European economic thought has become ensnared in the unreal framework of the following alternatives: *either* to develop heavy industry *or* to develop light industry and agriculture. But to juxtapose these as alternatives is false for two reasons. First, in the present situation we must take into full consideration the foreign trade position of the countries by which the rational proportions of the national economic structure is determined. It is particularly true for the small countries but greater countries cannot disregard this fact either. Second, the development of both agriculture and light industry required the complementary development of special branches of heavy industry, especially where their work is otherwise unduly burdensome or costly.

6. Hungarian experiences fully prove the author's point of view that "private-plot economy and other forms of auxiliary economy should be allowed greater development". However, it is not only in "the economically backward and poor areas" that they can play an important role, but even in a well-developed agrarian/industrial economy. A condition of the latter is that the household and other auxiliary economies should be integrated vertically into the big state or collective enterprises. That means that they must be provided with the most modern means of production and materials by the large enterprises and the processing and sale of the products of the small household enterprises should themselves be tackled on a large scale.

7. The author links the economic reforms with economic democracy. The omission of this link

had rather bad consequences in Eastern Europe. Reformist economists were generally thinking in terms of pure economic reform without considering political-social reforms at all, with the result that they did not win the support of the masses.

The author draws the conclusion that "It is therefore important to ensure that the people truly have the power to manage the affairs of the state and the enterprises. It is an important factor for preventing the 'evils' of bureaucracy. This is easy to say but very difficult to apply in practice. Experience has shown that the 'evil' of bureaucracy inevitably comes into existence in economic institutions, both in state administrative and self-management systems. Conceptions of how to eliminate bureaucracy proved illusory and later appeared as the apologetic ideology of the existing bureaucratic system. As a consequence, it is clear that only a comprehensive strategy of democracy can ensure the genuine rule of the working people. The main pillars of this strategy are, in my opinion, the following: workers' control, workers' participation, self-management, producers' associations, autonomous trade unions. I would be very glad if a seminal discussion could emerge from the very interesting theses of Mr. Su Shaozhi.

V

Some Comments
Michael Barratt Brown

The opening up of discussions between socialists in the West and leading representatives of the Chinese Communist Party can only be welcomed. This paper is especially welcome because of its frankness and self-critical approach to China's problems. Nobody who has visited China in the last two or three years can have missed either the tumult of re-thinking of the experience of China since 1949 going on among wide sections of the Chinese people or by the immensity of the changes made over the last thirty years. For those who know India, for example, the contrast is overwhelming in terms of health, nutrition, housing, education and purposive social activity. What is more it is not difficult for even a non-Chinese speaker on a short visit to recognise that economic advance has involved at least six elements which most of us would recognise as socialist.

a. a start to the re-integration of manual and mental labour;
b. the beginning of the ending of the antithesis of town and country;
c. a much improved status and position of women;
d. popular participation in management;

e. reversal of extreme specialisation in work and in studying;

f. a few early steps towards free supply of goods and services.

It is with all these thoughts clearly in mind that I offer the following rather critical observations of Su Shaozhi's statement. These are set out in the form of questions to the author because it is not at all my intention to arrogate to myself the right to make prescriptions for Chinese economic development on the basis of theoretical study and experience gained almost wholly within capitalist economic formations, and with so slight an acquaintance with China as I have.

The first question related to the period of the "great leap forward" (1956-59) and the period of the "great cultural revolution" (1966-1976). These are regarded as "set backs, when the development of the national economy was disrupted and valuable time was lost". Were there no benefits from the first period which saw the establishment of the communes and the second period when, with all its excesses, a possibly irreversible challenge was posed to those "evils of bureaucracy" which the author repeatedly warns against?

The second question follows: if, as the author asserts, the mistake in those two periods was to emphasise the continuing existence of "class struggle as the principal contradiction of socialism", why is there is still a need to "practise democratic centralism", i.e. where the "state power of the dictatorship of the proletariat led by the working class and based on the worker peasant alliance", is still exercised by a small group of leaders of the Chinese

Communist Party which can make massive "U-turns" in policy without prior discussion among the people?

The third question concerns the relationship between the Communist Party Committees and the democratic management of industrial and commercial enterprises or agricultural communes. How do the democratically elected workers' congresses operate "under the leadership of the Party Committee" and what is meant by the "under the leadership of the Party Committee" and what is meant by the "guided form" of their "role as an organ of power, of the staff and workers, to manage the enterprise . . .".

The fourth question relates to the new emphasis on material incentives "to each according to his work . . . he who does not work neither shall he eat." Does this imply a reduction in the beginnings of free supply not only in health and education but in public transport, central heating etc.?

The fifth question follows: what is the implication of "encouraging a part of the people and regions to become well off first as a result of receiving more income for more work? By what means will work be evaluated? What account will be taken of different levels of capital equipment at the disposal of workers in different enterprises or regions?

A sixth set of questions follows likewise. What is meant by "recognis(ing) the regulating role of the law of value *to a certain extent* and permit(ting) a certain degree of competition" (my emphasis — MBB). Is the law of value taken to mean that the value of any commodity is the amount of labour socially necessary or the labour time socially necessary for its production? If so, how is socially necessary labour time being measured? If prices are being used to equate the using up of real resources through competitive supply and demand, what are the distributive effects of major variations in necessary labour time around the social average?

The seventh set of questions relates, therefore, to administrative decisions on prices. The author quotes two recent Central Committee documents which "include raising the purchasing prices of farm products". What discussion led up to such a decision? Has there been any attempt to work out and publish "shadow prices" based on dated labour inputs and particularly to make available information on the respective sources in industry and agriculture of the 25 per cent accumulation rate?

The eighth question is a deep theoretical question about production relations and productive forces which has many practical implications. The author emphasises that economic laws must be obeyed and particularly that "production relations must be suited to the nature of the production forces; no attempt is to be made to change the mode of production relations prematurely and overtake the productive forces". Yet later on he writes that "whether a mode of the ownership of the means of production is good or bad should not be judged by its degree of public ownership; it should be judged by whether it can promote the development of the productive forces". Which comes first then, given a wide range of forms of ownership in the Chinese economy, ranging from individual through co-operative to state and not excluding "joint ventures of Chinese and foreign investment" (presumably private capitalist)? What will be the effect of the latter on socialist principles of self-management? It appears that the author is making an overall comparison of China's generally low level of productive forces and the inappropriateness, therefore, of advanced socialist forms of ownership, or at least of making them universal.

But this leads to a final question. This last question concerns the nature of the productive forces which China proposes to adopt in her modernisation programme and particularly in the utilisation of advanced foreign (presumably capitalist) technology. What adaptations do Chinese engineers and planners propose to make to technologies that incorporate a division of labour that is alienating but suits the accumulation of private capital — e.g. the separation of mental and manual labour, deskilling etc.? Even more seriously, what popular discussion is taking place about the priorities between the typical products of Western capitalist technology — private cars, washing machines, TV sets — and of the provision of public transport, public services, social activities and entertainments which the West has neglected?

VI

A Short Reply

Su Shaozhi

Through the efforts of Ken Coates, I received in succession, letters from Wlodzimierz Brus, Michael Barratt Brown, John Eaton and Andras Hegedüs. In these letters, they made comments on and raised questions about certain points in the paper I presented at the 1980 *Socialism in the World* round table conference, entitled *Some Questions in China's Socialist Economic Construction*. For this, I would like to express my gratitude.

I am very much in favour of the view they have expressed concerning the holding of free and frank discussions among socialists of all countries. This kind of discussion is of crucial importance to the enhancement of understanding between socialists of different countries and the promotion of socialism in the world.

Professor Brus' comment was extremely helpful to me. His remark — "there are no ideal solutions, that is to say that by opting for a particular solution we should be aware also of the possible negative consequences which have to be minimised" is indeed of vital importance. Due to the limits of space, my paper lacked analysis in this aspect. The questions he raised by way of example are ones which have been and are still being much discussed among Chinese economists. In view of their complexity, to tackle them, special articles have to be written. In practice, we also see things in this light. For example, at the Fourth Session of the Fifth National People's Congress, talking about the economic readjustment in the past year, Premier Zhao Ziyang said that we should not only take note of the striking successes scored, but also the fact that the latent dangers in our national economy have not been completely eliminated. In commenting on China's economic prospects, while analysing the strengths of China's economic development, he also referred to the weaknesses. All in all, Professor Brus' view is of significance whether it is from the point of view of theory and practice, or from the point of view of methodology.

Almost all the professors talked about the question of periodization of China's economic development since the founding of the People's Republic. The periodization I gave in my paper is essentially, as Professor Hegedüs suggested, based on the changes in political direction and the economic policies involved, so as to facilitate analysis and the summing up of experience. The periodization given in "The Resolution on Certain Questions in the History of Our Party since the Founding of the People's Republic of China" adopted by the Sixth Plenary Session of the Eleventh Central Committee of the Communist Party of China (hereinafter referred to as the Resolution) in June 1981, is also more or less like this. To analyse further, the first of the five stages referred to in my paper is concerned with what Professor Hegedüs termed "changes in the institutional system", because it was in this stage that the transition from new democracy to socialism was realised. From then on, China entered the initial stage of socialist society. The few stages that followed all appertain to the initial stage of socialist society and are only differentiated from one another according to changes in political directions and the economic policies involved. Of course, when the economic and political reforms currently under way in our country are completed, there may be certain specific changes in the institutional system also.

To John Eaton, the period of restoration of the national economy and the period of the First Five-Year Plan in China seemed something of a "golden age". He also put forward the view that "perhaps there is still something to learn from these early years following Liberation in 1949". Certainly, China obtained great successes in that stage and indeed there is still something to learn from those years. There are also many people in China to whom that stage seems a "golden age". Yet I hold that the successes obtained in that stage were predicated on the prevailing objective and subjective conditions and not everything then can be said to be perfect. For example, as is pointed out in my paper, there existed the shortcoming of mechanically copying the experience of other countries without giving full consideration to China's actual conditions. Some of the errors and serious mistakes committed in the stages that followed can also be traced to that stage. Besides, the objective and subjective conditions in the 1980s have changed tremendously from those of the fifties. I am of the view that the model of the fifties does not hold the key to the solution of problems of the eighties.

Michael Barratt Brown asked whether or not there were benefits from the period of the Great Leap Forward and the period of the "cultural revolution". I hold that in a socialist country, owing to the superiority of the socialist system itself and the efforts of all the labouring people, though errors and even serious mistakes occur in certain stages, social production will still undergo development to a certain extent. The political directions, and the economic policies involved, of a certain period should be evaluated in their totality. The Resolution correctly pointed out, the "cultural revolution" was "a grave error comprehensive in magnitude and protracted in duration". It was "initiated by a leader labouring under a misapprehension and capitalised on by counter-revolutionary cliques", and "led to domestic turmoil and brought catastrophe to the Party, the state and the whole people". It added, "Of course, it was essential to take proper account of certain undesirable phenomena that undoubtedly existed in Party and state organisms and to remove them by correct measures in conformity with the Constitution, the laws and the Party Constitution. But on no account should the theories and methods of the 'cultural revolution' have been applied." Although not as comprehensive in magnitude or protracted in duration as in the "cultural revolution", a grave error existed in the guiding principles of the "Great Leap Forward". The Resolution pointed out, "After the general line was formulated, the 'Great Leap Forward' and the movement for rural people's communes were initiated without careful investigation and study and without prior experimentation. As a result, 'Left' errors, characterised by excessive targets, the issuing of arbitrary directions, boastfulness and the stirring up of a 'communist wind', spread unchecked throughout the country.

In other words, an error was also committed in the movement for rural people's communes in disregarding the level of the development of productive forces in China's rural areas. The experiments now carried out in certain counties and districts in China, in relinquishing the people's commune as an organisation which "integrates government administration with commune management", and which is "big in size" and supposedly "of a more developed socialist nature" and turning it into a township, a mere level of government, has proved to be effective.

Michael Barratt Brown, John Eaton and Andras Hegedüs all put forward views on the relationship between production relations and productive forces. It was not my intention in my paper to say that the low level of the development of productive forces is generally not suited to the advanced socialist forms of ownership of the means of production. What I meant to say was, given the existence of multiple levels of productive forces in China, accordingly, there should be multiple forms of ownership of the means of production. On this question, the Resolution clearly pointed out, "The state economy and the collective economy are the basic forms of the Chinese economy. The working people's individual economy within certain prescribed limits is a necessary complement to public economy." Joint ventures of Chinese and foreign investment are one of this wide range of forms of production relations.

The view put forward by Professor Brus on the relationship between market mechanism and central planning is enlightening. After two years of experimentation, we have come to understand deeply, as Professor Brus put it, that the "role of the market mechanism, in principle, can be reconciled with central planning. But it is not an easy job". The relationship between the two is still under discussion among Chinese economists. The Resolution asserted that, "it is necessary to have a planned economy and at the same time give play to the supplementary, regulatory role of the market on the basis of public ownership." It was in this sense that I wrote in my paper, "it is necessary to acknowledge the regulating role of the law of value to a certain extent and permit a certain degree of competition." In commenting on the correct understanding and handling of the relationship between planning and market regulation at the recent Fourth Session of the Fifth National People's Congress, Premier Zhao Ziyang clearly pointed out, "while upholding the planned socialist economy, (it is necessary to) give scope to the supplementary role of regulation through the market and fully take into account and utilize the law of value when working out state plans". This can be said to represent the views of the majority of people in China's economic circles.

A question ensuing from the last point is reform

of the price structure, a question which both Professor Brus and Michael Barratt Brown mentioned. In theory, it is relatively clear that in order to bring into play the role of market mechanisms, it is necessary first of all, to change the old price structure, because the old administratively set prices have for long failed to adjust to the changes in labour productivity of different products, divorcing market prices from value (price of production) — totally at variance with economic principles and failing to provide reliable feedback. In theory, I am all in favour of reform of the price structure, a reform which should aim at eventually enabling the retail price to be proportionate to value (price of production). Yet in practice, it is a very complicated task which should be carried out step by step after meticulous computation.

Professor Hegedüs made comments on the relationship between agriculture, light industry and heavy industry. Recently, the Western press has come up with reports suggesting that China is indecisive in this regard. The fact is, in the light of the experience accumulated in the past thirty-two years since the founding of the People's Republic, we have been clear all along that to accelerate the development of agriculture and give priority to the development of consumer goods industry does not amount to neglect of heavy industry. Instead, such policies call for the further adjustment of the service orientation of heavy industry. That is to say, the development of heavy industry should serve first of all the development of agriculture and light industry.

Both Professor Brus and Michael Barratt Brown

offered observations on the questions of material incentives and China's distribution policy. In this context, Professor Brus admonished us not to go from one extreme to the other. I think in a socialist society, neither the economic nor the social principles should be ignored. In order to bring into play the initiative and creativity of the labouring people and continuously raise labour productivity, material incentives, the principle "to each according to his work" and income differentials must all be given due recognition and a part of the people and regions be allowed to become well off first as a result of receiving more income for more work. Yet, the income differentials developed on the basis of common prosperity should not be permitted to become so wide as to lead to polarisation and the occurrence of exploitation. At the same time, on the basis of the development of production and with the rise in individual income, it is necessary to gradually increase collective social welfare. The attempt to re-emphasise material incentives and the principle of to each according to his work, is mainly aimed at eliminating the so-called unbreakable rice bowl and the phenomena of equalitarianism, and "everyone eating from the same big pot" which prevailed before 1976 and which up till now still has not become extinct. This is because such phenomena run counter to the socialist distribution principle of to each according to his labour, corrupt the minds of the labouring people, and are not conducive to the increase in labour productivity and development of production. None of the reasonable items of collective welfare such as free medical care in the civil service and state enterprises, co-operative medical care in the countryside, and low rentals and public transport fares is renounced.

All the professors mentioned questions relating to democratic participation, opposition to bureaucratism, and economic and political reform. I treasure greatly and agree completely with their views concerning democracy. As a Chinese saying has it, "the whole of my heart is captured". I am very happy to inform them that the Resolution unequivocally stated, "A fundamental task of the socialist revolution is gradually to establish a highly democratic socialist political system" and the objective of the Communist Party in the new historical period is "to turn China step by step into a powerful modern socialist country with a high level of democracy and culture". At the recently concluded Fourth Session of the Fifth National People's Congress, Premier Zhao Ziyang emphasised the need to overcome the tendency of bureaucratism both in politics and economic management. Just as Professor Brus said, "it is not enough to recognise verbally the indispensability of democratic participation, an effort must be made to chart the ways of implementation of the principle". There is a lot of work we have to do to obtain a high level of democracy. Yet a good beginning has been made on the route of democratisation. It is a route which we will continue to follow.

VII
Science Technology and Democratisation in Socialist Development Strategies*

Su Shaozhi

A TENTATIVE DISCOURSE ON THE CHINESE ROAD TO MODERNISATION

The objective the Chinese Communist Party is striving to attain in the new historical period is to turn China step by step into a powerful socialist country with modern agriculture, industry, national defence and science and technology and with a high level of democracy and culture. The development goal to be reached by the end of this century is to "enable everyone to be comparatively well-off". Yet, how to turn this general goal of endeavour into more specific ones? What road and steps will have to be undertaken towards its fulfilment? To answer these questions, it is necessary to continue to free oneself from all the old and new constraints, to find out clearly and accurately China's conditions and the relationship between various factors in economic activites and to carry out an in-depth study of China's economic and social development strategy. In other words, it is to study the question of the Chinese road to moder-

*Paper delivered at the Round Table 1981 of "Socialism in the World" International Conference, held in Cavtat, Yugoslavia, from 21 to 26 September 1981.

nisation.

In the past, the developing countries, in setting their development goals, often took the industrialised countries as their development model, with the emphasis on Gross National Product (GNP) growth to achieve national affluence and prosperity as their development strategy's general orientation. This kind of development strategy has come to be known as the Conventional Development Strategy (CDS).

Economists and sociologists have become increasingly aware that GNP as a measurement of a nation's economic development and achievements has serious drawbacks and limitations. For example, GNP does not measure certain subjective and objective factors that are very important to social welfare, and therefore cannot reflect correctly the consumption level or economic welfare that the people of a nation enjoy. The conventional development strategy adopted by some developing countries to blindly seek GNP growth regardless of their national condition in order to catch up with and surpass certain other countries has serious drawbacks in practice. Seeking impractical development goals often results in disproportions in the economy, irrationality in the economic structure and social problems such as increase in unemployment, consumer goods shortages and a marked disparity between the rich and the poor.

Owing to the disappointing results in the implementation of the Conventional Development Strategy, in recent years, the goal of development strategies has been changed into guaranteeing the more effective satisfaction of basic human needs while increasing production. To meet this requirement, various Alternative Development Strategies (ADS) have been extensively and actively explored. The characteristic of these types of development strategies is that their strategic goal is no longer the obtainment of GNP growth only, but they also attach equal importance to other factors while endeavouring to increase GNP. Some hold that it is necessary to pay serious attention to guaranteeing the more effective satisfaction of basic human needs or minimum human needs. Others suggest that the emphasis should be put on the physical quality of life. Still others argue that it is imperative to set store by growth with equity. Therefore, statistically it is no longer sufficient just to have GNP figures. Recently, new indices have been extensively sought for to achieve more effective measurement in these respects; or GNP is adjusted in accordance with the requirements in these respects; or else these new indices are used together with GNP per capita (or NNP per capita). The Alternative Development Strategies call for additional measurement systems.

Among the more commonly used ones of these are: the Sustainable Measure of Economic Welfare (MEW) put forward by US economists William D. Nordhaus and James Tobin; the Physical Quality of Life Index (PQLI) put forward by the US economist Morris D. Morris; the the ASHA index formulated by the American Social Health Association. All these measurement systems represent a big step forward from the national accounts system consisting of GNP and NNP.

The Conventional Development Strategy has

already proved unsuccessful in practice. China will certainly not repeat this strategy. In order to formulate a sound economic and social development strategy that conforms to China's actual conditions and is practicable and of benefit to the masses, it is essential to make an in-depth study of the following four major questions: socialism, China's conditions, modern science and technology, and democratisation. On the basis of such a study, the long term goal of our endeavour and the development goal by the end of the century should gradually be broken down into specific ones and observations be made regarding the formulation of a measurement system for social development that conforms to China's characteristics and is internationally comparable.

SOCIALISM

China is a developing socialist country. In formulating her economic and social development strategy, the most important and invariable principle is to persist in following the socialist road.

The material and technological base of socialism is socialised mass production. The basic characteristics of the socialist relationship of production are: public ownership of the means of production, the elimination of exploitation and distribution according to labour. The aim of socialist production is the maximum satisfaction of everyone's material and cultural needs. The superstructure of socialism is a high level of democracy and culture. The general goals of socialism are the immense development of productive forces, great progress in politics and culture and finally the realisation of Communism — the association of free men under which all class differences are eliminated and the principle of "from each according to his ability and to each according to his needs" prevails.

China's economic and social development strategy is by no means simply to seek high speed or to catch up with and surpass certain other countries in economic development, but to foster its socialist character and enable it to follow the socialist general orientation.

For this purpose, in formulating China's development strategy the following three points must be taken into account:

1. It should be conducive to the development of productive forces, the consolidation of socialist relations of production and the realisation of social equity. Neither the economic principle nor the social principle should be over-emphasised at the expense of the other.

In order to bring into play the initiative and creativity of the labouring people and to raise labour productivity constantly, the principle of "to each according to his labour" must be adhered to, income differentials accepted and some people allowed to become rich before others. This kind of income differential has developed on the basis of the common prosperity of the labouring people and is not permitted to become too big to result in polarisation and the emergence of exploitation. At the same time, on the basis of production growth, while personal income is increased, collective social welfare should gradually be augmented as well.

To suit the nature and level of the development

of productive forces, the form of the relations of production and of labour remuneration should be permitted to be diversified provided that exploitation will not emerge. At present the co-existence of the public sector, collective economy and self-employment within certain limits is conducive to production growth and increase in employment.

2. It should aim at meeting to the extent possible the material and cultural needs of all the members of the society. Neither the material side nor the intellectual side should be neglected.

The development goal of socialism is the emancipation and well-being of the people and the maximum satisfaction of people's material and cultural needs. "Maximum" refers to the level permitted by production growth and does not mean without limitations. Material and cultural needs according to Marx include the need for survival, for enjoyment and for development. The need for survival is man's basic need or minimum need. The need for enjoyment and development, however, includes improvement in the quality of life. All these needs have two sides to them one material and the other intellectual.

From the material side, man's primary needs consist of eight main categories: food, clothing, shelter, daily necessities, means of transport, education, health care and recreation. The ratio between these categories thus constitutes the structure of consumption. This structure of consumption does not always remain the same. With the rise of economic and cultural levels and increase in working people's income, the scope and structure of consumption will change accordingly. For example, as production grows the proportion of food consumption will decrease whereas the consumption of durable goods and the proportion of education and recreation requirements will relatively increase.

With a view to continuously meeting the ever-increasing material and cultural needs of the people, China's construction should be oriented from one that over-emphasises the development of heavy industry — "taking steel as the key link" — to one that lays stress on the growth of the production of consumer goods and ensures that heavy industry mainly serves the production needs of consumer goods, the production of means of production coordinates with that of the consumer goods, and the structure of production dovetails with that of consumption. This is a construction policy that will enable the economy to embark on the road of healthy development.

China's development strategy should not only give high priority to the production of consumer goods, it should also specify the level of consumption each stage should attain. For example, with respect to food, the annual per capita consumption of grain, meat, milk, eggs and the average daily per capita intake of calories may be specified. With housing, per capita square metres of floor-space, with education, illiteracy rate, number of university students per thousand persons, with health care, morbidity rate, mortality rate, average life expectancy, number of doctors and hospital beds per thousand persons and other even more specific targets may all be set. Also specific requirements should be set for the development of heavy industry towards the fulfilment of these targets. Besides, in order to guarantee the satisfaction of the needs for enjoyment and development, not only the material goods must be available to meet these needs, there should also be a certain amount of leisure time. Activities that are beneficial to man's physical and mental health and help to raise his cultural level may be conducted in a gradually increasing amount of leisure time.

In a socialist society, on the basis of the improvement in the material life, the intellectual life will undergo steady development. It takes many forms including political, scientific, artistic, cultural life and that prevailing in man's various ethical relationships. In short, it is embodied in the democratisation of political and social life, social stability, justice and equity and highly developed social morality. Although the material standard of living in the developed capitalist countries is relatively high, yet there exist social unrest and immense intellectual deprivation. A "sense of security" is lacking in political and social life. People are not "free from fear" and thus cannot enjoy real happy lives. In the Italian society, for example, there exist four evils, crimes, drug-taking, terrorism and Maffia, which endanger the normal life of the people and cause social crises. In a socialist society, social problems like drug-taking, prostitution, terrorism and so on are non-existent. Yet the socialist society has not ridded itself completely of the vestiges and influence of the old society it has superseded. Therefore, social problems like crimes, traffic accidents etc. and "social indices" like crime rate, traffic accident rate etc, still give cause for concern. The development goal should also take into consideration the requirement for the lowering of these indices and the gradual establishment of ethical relationships based on Communist morality and the cultivation of a new social ethos.

3. It should avoid the defects developed in the modernisation process of the capitalist countries.

The various defects that have developed in the process of modernisation of the capitalist countries have drawn increasing concern. In the latter half of the 1970s, there emerged the "post-industrial era" movement in the West. This is a school of thought that advocates departure from the Western modern industrial era which is fraught with waste, pollution and intranquility and entry into an ideal era characterised by frugality, cleanliness, stability and equity.

The major defects developed in the Western industrialisation process this school of thought points towards are very much worthy of our attention and should be avoided.

The first defect is the problem of enormous waste. Capitalism, owing to its decadent nature, has developed into a consumer society that must rely on waste and stimulus for prosperity. It is characterised by "massive production, massive abuse and massive waste". For example, the car which signifies an extremely wasteful way of living has become an evil in Western societies. Travelling in vehicles at too high a speed also does not conform with economic principles. In the Western "civilised life", the annual renewal of cars, watches, styles of clothing and other things for ostentatious purposes is by no means necessary for survival and is not even relevant to enjoyment or development. It is this kind of consumer society that we should try our best to avoid.

The second defect is environmental pollution and upset of the ecological balance. With the rapid pace of industrialisation and urbanisation, industrial wastes and over-use of chemical fertilisers and pesticides have resulted in serious environmental pollution and ecological imbalance. Industrial waste water and waste residue have polluted water sources, rivers, lakes and even the seas, jeopardising the lives of fish and birds and poisoning men and animals. What is more, the use of super oil-tankers and accidents in off-shore oil drilling have caused oil pollution in the sea. Nuclear wastes produced in the process of nuclear power generatimon and accidents have led to radioactive pollution. Industrial exhaust has increased the carbon-dioxide content in the atmosphere affecting the climate of the whole world. The burning of sulphur-bearing fuels has led to acid-rains which corrode buildings and destroy forests, lakes and fisheries. The pollution caused by chemical fertilisers and pesticides like DDT is also extremely serious and has a considerable impact on the ecological system. In the West, the correlation between the increase in the degree of industrial and agricultural development and the worsening of pollution problems and ecological imbalance has already aroused widespread concern from economists, ecologists and sociologists. Even in China's preliminary industrialisation process, problems in this respect are becoming increasingly serious. Much attention must be paid to them in the formulation of China's develoment strategy.

The third defect is the waste of natural resources and their gradual depletion. In order to obtain maximum profits, the capitalist countries have resorted to indiscriminate, abusive and wasteful methods in the exploitation and use of resources. It is by no means accidental that there have appeared the energy and other non-fuel resource crises in the West. Attention must be paid so that China's development strategy does not follow the same road. The West is beginning to pay attention to the application of solar energy or renewable energy and organic farming — a switch to organic fertilisers, biological control and soil conservation. In China, due to poor management and bad economic results, the problems of waste of resources like energy and forest is already very grave and should draw our serious concern.

The fourth defect is social problems. Western modernisation with its over-emphasis on pursuing material goals has resulted in social problems like over-crowded cities, increase in unemployment, polarisation between the rich and poor, moral degeneration, increased alienation in men's relationship with one another, intellectual deprivation, decadence and increase in crimes. In China's modernisation process problems like these absolutely cannot be allowed to emerge.

In their development and modernisation processes, certain developing countries have relied excessively on foreign capital and as a result are heavily burdened with debts and even subjected to the economic and political control of transnational corporations. This is something that China should also guard against and avoid. We shall actively promote economic co-operation and technical exchanges with other countries and use foreign capital in a rational way but all these should be based on independence and self-reliance.

CHINA'S CONDITIONS

Just as Marxism must be combined with the realities of each country to win the victory of revolution, the development strategy of a country must proceed from its actual conditions to yield positive results. China is a developing socialist country with a vast territory, a big population, and a long history. And it has its unique historical and cultural traditions. It is important to make an in-depth study of China's conditions and proceeding from there to formulate a development strategy suitable to the Chinese situation.

The conditions of a country are multi-dimensional and call for extensive and in-depth research for their clear and thorough understanding. I agree with the view expressed in the *Note on Holding a Seminar on the Question of Economic and Social Development Strategies* which says, "Our country's conditions should not only include its natural environment, i.e., national land resource, population (both as a source of manpower and as consumers), the state of economic development in all aspects, such as the level of development of science, education and culture, all important social and other aspects like the state of various social relations and contradictions should also be taken into account. They should not only include the old China's heritage, the changes that took place between the founding of the People's Republic and the end of the Cultural Revolution, but also the changes during the four and more years after the end of the Cultural Revolution. In investigating China's conditions, it is necessary to try and understand China's capabilities and examine the various potentials for development as well as all the advantages and disadvantages in tapping these potentials."[1] Naturally, a thorough understanding of these conditions can only be the result of extensive and in-depth investigations and studies and cannot be obtained instantly. Yet, attention should be focused on the following major aspects.

China has a population of 1,000 million, of which 800 million are in the countryside. These are China's basic conditions. These basic conditions show that China's development strategy should give prime consideration to the development of agriculture and be designed to cater well for the needs of people's livelihood, especially the people living in the countryside that make up 80 per cent of the population, to solve their food and clothing problems and enable them to lead a life that is being constantly improved. This question concerns the overall stability of our country. Secondly, they indicate that China's development strategy should attach due importance to the question of full employment i.e. the question of the full utilisation of existing human resources. Thirdly, they suggest that the development of agriculture

1. Policy Research Dept. of the State Scientific Commission and other five units: "Note on Holding a Seminar on the Question of Economic and Social Development Strategies" (12 Feb. 1981, p.4).

should have its emphasis on studying ways to raise agricultural labour productivity and commodity rate of agricultural products. This concerns the important question of meeting the needs for subsistence and other needs of the people of cities and towns and lessening the reliance on imported agricultural products.

While China is relatively rich in natural resources, it lacks adequate funds and technology for their development in the short term, thus the resources that may be used for production and construction in the immediate future are rather limited. This is another important aspect of China's conditions. This shows that in setting China's development goal, the rate of accumulation and growth rate, it is essential to match them with our capabilities and not to go beyond the realm of the possibility of the supply of resources within the planned period, which include among other things, raw materials, fuel, power, technology, technical personnel, managerial personnel and skilled labour. Secondly it shows the necessity of the measured use of foreign capital and introduction of advanced foreign technologies when domestic funds are lacking. Yet, in so doing, it is important to consider whether or not the corresponding domestic scale of capital construction, technical capabilities, infrastructure, and the supply of energy and raw materials are overstretched. Thirdly it shows that human investment for raising the population's quality should become an important component part of China's development strategy in order to greatly increase the cultural, technical and managerial level of the whole population.

Before liberation, China's industry was very backward. During the thirty years and more since the founding of the People's Republic, industry has undergone no small development. In 1980, its total fixed assets calculated at original prices amounted to over 410 billion *yuan*. Yet its present problems lie in all-round heavy waste and poor economic returns on the part of the enterprise. The labour productivity and profit rate of many enterprises, while falling behind that of the world's advanced level, up till now have still not attained their own past records. Therefore, in the present economic endeavour, it is necessary that the method of seeking state investment, building new factories and enlarging production scales for production growth be changed. Future production growth shall not mainly be obtained through building new factories or increasing the scale of capital construction, but through bringing into full play the role of existing enterprises, their gradual integration and more intensive management. In the coming fives years or even more, except for certain necessary projects to strengthen the weak links of the economy, like energy and transport, basically, there will be no more construction of new factories. The limited funds and materials will first be used in tapping the potentials, innovation and technical transformation of the existing enterprises. In China, the machinery industry which provides equipment for all other sectors of the national economy has already attained a considerable scale of development. This is something that distinguishes China from some other developing countries. China's modernisation should proceed from protecting and developing her own machinery industry. The introduction of foreign equipment is intended to develop but not to weaken it. The problems of China's machinery industry are: systemic disorder, unstreamlined management, compartmentalisation, low technological level, low efficiency and irrational structure. With the machinery industry therefore, the present emphasis should be put on reorganisation and technical transformation.

After the founding of the People's Republic, China's economic system was modelled exactly on the highly centralised planning system of a foreign country. This system's defect is its overcentralisation and rigidity. The serious mistakes made since the latter half of 1950s and the sabotage of the Lin Biao/Jiang Qing counter-revolutionary clique not only have greatly impaired China's economic and social development but also brought about irrationalities in the economic system, economic structure, enterprise organisation and problems like ecological imbalance, sectoral disproportions, dislocation between production and demand, low economic returns and big waste. It is imperative therefore that China's development strategy should include a programme of economic reform, for the gradual rationalisation of the economic structure, the economic system and enterprise organisation so as to achieve balanced development and stable growth of the national economy.

From the intellectual side, the impact of the historical and national heritage on the character of China's economic and social development should also be fully taken into account. Qualities like industry, courage and frugality that the labouring people have acquired in the age-long struggle against nature and rulers and the tradition of mutual help among the labouring people and good family relations are all conducive to social and economic development and to preventing the corrosive effect of capitalism and should all be developed and given a socialist content. As for the vestige of long-time feudal despotism in ideology and politics and the influence of bourgeois ideology, things like patriarchal behaviour, personal arbitrariness, personality cult, "one man's forum",* bureaucratism, the forces of inertia on the part of the small producer, and disparagement of science and technology, and manual labour, they are the big obstacles to economic development and must be removed.

Modern Science and Technology

Science is a motive force in history. Science and technology are productive forces on which economic development must depend. Advanced modern science and technology in particular, have put large quantities of equipment in place of labour, causing the shooting up of labour productivity, plummeting of production costs, rapid increase in the variety of products and constant quality improvement. It is by no means fortuitous that in the formulation of a country's development programme the goal has always been to obtain advanced modern science and technology.

---

*One man alone has the say.

However, like all things, modern advanced science and technology also have two sides to them. Their problems are as follows;

1. The modern industry's ability to 'absorb' man-power is weak because the modern industry has a high organic constituent of capital and with the increase in investment, the demand for living labour relatively drops. This is at variance with the solution called for in the developing countries where the employment pressure is very high.

2. Modern industry requires a great deal of investment and trained personnel with high scientific and technical qualifications. This is also in contradiction with the state of affairs in the developing countries where the levels of culture and accumulation are rather low.

3. Modern industry consumes a great deal of energy and other resources and is liable to bring about serious pollution problems and the problem of over-crowded cities.

It goes without saying that in order to realise China's modernisation programme, in practice a high value must be attached to the study and development of science and technology and attention be paid to the introduction of the modern technologies of other countries. Yet the science and technology policy as part of China's economic and social development strategy must conform with the socialist aims of production and proceed from China's conditions. The question now is how to truly bring into play the role of science and technology and turn them into a great dynamic force in increasing social and economic benefits and developing the economy. Therefore, it is necessary that the science and technology policy as part of China's development strategy take into consideration the following special points:

1. It should give priority to the production of consumer goods and the development of agriculture and the countryside.

2. It should give full play to China's advantages and avoid the disadvantages and study the ways and means as to achieve the most rational utilisation of China's various resources including the human resources. It should give priority to the development of labour intensive industries instead of capital intensive ones and those sectors whose products are in great demand, needing little investment while bringing quick returns.

3. Science and technology must first serve the current needs of economic development. Advanced technology indicates the orientation of technological progress and is something we certainly cannot make light of studying. But the emphasis of our studies should be put on appropriate technologies and efforts should be exerted to master them well. It is important to distinguish between the abstract concept of science being advanced and the concepts of technology being appropriate during a certain period and to a certain country. Before the use and promotion of certain technologies, it is crucial to consider whether or not they are appropriate rather than seeking blindly the advanced technologies, for appropriate technologies are the ones that will bring the real economic benefits to the user under the prevailing conditions of his country, whereas advanced technologies, advanced as they are, will only bring

certain losses if they are not suitable to the circumstances and arbitrarily used.[1] It is the same with importing technologies. For this reason, only some advanced technologies of structural importance will be employed if the conditions allow and if they can really increase social and economic benefits, whereas appropriate technologies will be used in the majority of cases. It is necessary that automatic, mechanised and semi-mechanised production and manual labour should all be developed with a view to fully utilising China's human resources and promoting production both in scope and in depth.

DEMOCRATISATION

Modernisation cannot simply be equated with industrialisation or economic growth but should at the same time include democratisation. In 1919, the main slogans put forward by the Chinese people in the New Culture Movement were centred on the promotion of Democracy and Science. Democracy is indeed indispensable to modernisation. Without it, there is no socialism, no modernisation.

Modernisation certainly should include the development of science and technology, education, management methods and others so as to raise labour productivity and greatly expand productive forces. Democratisation is of great significance to all the things mentioned above, and thus to

1. Yu Guangyuan, "The Importance of Research into the Integration of Science and Technology with Economic and Social Development", Hangzhou World Economy Session.

economic development. This is because of the following reasons:

1. The initiative and creativity of the labouring people are important to raising labour productivity and greatly expanding productive forces and it is only through democratisation to enable the labouring people to become true masters of the enterprise, society and state that their initiative and creativity can be brought into full play.

2. If economic development is to be accelerated, things must be done in conformity with the objective economic laws. Yet the understanding of these laws is not as a result of the brain-racking effort of a genius but acquired by tens of millions of labouring people from practice. It is only through democratisation that arbitrariness can be avoided, interference from the 'left' or 'right' eliminated and experience correctly summed up.

3. In a socialist country "the classical social impediments to economic development" (Brus) i.e. such factors as the anarchic state of production, the periodic crises of over-production and so on have been gradually eliminated. But the vestiges of feudal despotism and capitalism left over by the old society, such as over-concentration of power in the hands of a few persons, "one man's forum", arbitrariness of economic decisions, muddleheadedness and incompetencies and bureaucratism which is callous to the hardships and difficulties of the masses become obstacles to economic development. Democratisation is a good remedy for these defects.[1]

1. Su Shaozhi, "Economic Development and Democratisation", Selected Writing in Studies of Marxism, No. 8 Ch. 2.

The development of science and technology on the other hand extensively eliminates ignorance of the masses, facilitates the accumulation and dissemination of knowledge and leads to a big increase in the number of intellectuals and the use of the communication media in the society and even in the world as a whole, thus accelerating the process of democratisation. Democratisation and modernisation therefore, are one and the same process. They promote each other and develop hand in hand.

In a country such as China which had for thousands of years been under the sway of feudalism, although the feudal economic base or political system no longer exists, the vestiges of feudal despotism and their ideological impact will remain for a long time. They impede the advantage of the socialist system being brought into full play and become serious obstacles on China's road to modernisation. Therefore, in formulating China's economic and social development strategy, democratisation should become a question deserving priority consideration. It should consist of various important measures designed to develop socialist democracy, like establishing and perfecting various organs including People's Congresses at all levels, Staff/Worker Representative Congresses in all work units through which the people may truly and effectively exercise their rights to administer political, economic and social affairs and various supervisory and procuratorial systems instituted to bring into perfection the democratic administration of state, society and enterprise. Effective measures should be taken to turn the various democratic rights of the people as provided in the Constitution into realities, and efforts should continue to be made to step up socialist legislative work so as to perfect China's present laws and enable them to offer better protection to the citizen in the exercise of his democratic rights. In the Resolution on Certain Questions in the History of the Party Since the Founding of the People's Republic of China adopted by the Central Committee of CPC, it is clearly pointed out that, "a fundamental task of the socialist revolution is gradually to establish a highly democratic socialist political system."

A question worth studying in this context is how the degree of democratisation is to be reflected statistically. Concerning the question of the labouring people's participation in the political and economic decision making processes, there is a statistic of some significance in Yugoslavia which may be used for our reference. In 1979, when Tito, the former President, was making a speech at a mass meeting in Belgrade organised by the Central Committee of the Yugoslavian Communist League, he said, "during the last general election of spring 1978, nearly 800,000 people were elected as members of the delegation, out of which over 53,000 delegates were elected to the Social-Political Community Skupstina at all levels. If the members of Worker's Councils, Self-Management Interest Community and various committee members of Local Communities are all added to the above figure, it would amount to over 1.2 million people participating in the political decision making process through the delegate system."[1] In 1979, Yugoslavia had a population of 21,968,000. This is to say about 18.3 per cent of the total population took a direct part in the political decision making process.

Since the convening of the Third Plenary Session of its Eleventh Central Committee, the Communist Party of China has charted a correct course for socialist modernisation which is suited to China's conditions. The question of how to formulate an economic and social development strategy in line with this correct course is still one that calls for a great deal of work.

---

1. Tito, "Selected Works of Tito (1974-1980)", Chinese edition by the People's Publishing House, page 403.

The Contributors

Su Shaozhi is Vice-Director of the Institute of Marxism-Leninism-Mao Zedong Thought under the Chinese Academy of Social Sciences and Professor of Economics at the Faculty of Economics, Beijing University.

Wlodzimierz Brus lectures in Soviet and East European Studies at the University of Oxford.

John Eaton is the author of *Political Economy,* the well-known textbook on Marxist economics. He worked in China after the Revolution.

Andras Hegedüs is a sociologist. He was prime minister of Hungary before the 1956 uprising.

Michael Barratt Brown is an economist. He is Principal of Northern College, Wentworth.
thern College.